GHOST NOTES

Ralph Burns

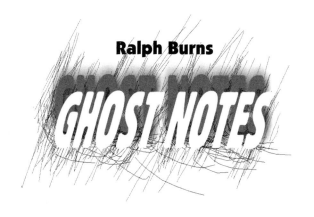

OBERLIN COLLEGE PRESS
Oberlin, Ohio

www.oberlin.edu/~ocpress

Publication of this book was supported in part by a grant from the Ohio Arts Council.

Ohio Arts Council
A STATE AGENCY
THAT SUPPORTS PUBLIC
PROGRAMS IN THE ARTS

Cover image: "Fra Angelico meets Ornette Coleman," Stephen Henriques, 1988.

Oil on canvas, $45^3/4$ x $44^1/4$

www.stephenhenriques.com

Private collection. Printed with permission.

Library of Congress Cataloging-in-Publication Data

Burns, Ralph
      Ghost Notes/ Ralph Burns.
      (The FIELD Poetry Series v. 10)
      I. Title. II. Series.

LCCN: 2001087317

ISBN: 0-932440-88-6 (pbk.)

CONTENTS

In Memory of W. O. Calhoun

I

Ghost Notes

for Danny Fletcher

I. Call and Response

1

Plumbline of disaster, shadow storage
    of the way thought travels, the opinion,
the sentiment, only assertion following silence,
    only a way of everlasting breathing,
a verb searching for grammar too devoted
    to making sense so that the self interrupts
with a final pitch. From stop to stop the mouth
    makes music by holding sound in a razz
mixed with spit, air pushing through idea
    to a new phrase, followed by a chill,
then riding on the other air. So the moment might live
    outside itself, lips vibrate against
the mouthpiece of the horn, the face blooms
    in concentration, the idea of interval.

2

Anoint the valves, they stick — my
    it is bright when you bring out your trumpet,
William, standing there, tapping your right
    foot, bent like a cricket at the knee, slouching.
Whoever hears your *Ode to Joy* hears your knocking
    then setting down of carrying
case, cradling of brass. Dizzy said it took
    his whole life to learn what not
to play but in one month you deny nothing,
    not even the feel of your embouchure,
who'd been in school all day. Lubricate the valves,
    once neighbors lifted up their heads
like lilies in the field, and wind rolled over
    the need to stay away.

3

It's beauty people fear, bright
      rose riding on Aunt Billie's forehead,
the way light makes green everything
      after her pickled okra, stubble
in the hands of day labor, calluses
      of a parade of things and
touching them without seeing
      or hearing without knowledge,
dumbstruck by a brooding need to define
      or look without a place
to grieve, beauty and not faith
      in truth in the light of justice —
just reach and nothing's there
      but what's there already.

4

William — where — is — your — horn,
    did you leave it in math class again
with Fibonacci's sequence, flaring
    bell, flex and curve in sunlight leaning
at a forty-five degree angle,
    your teacher Mr. Fletcher having cranked
open the classroom window with an allen wrench,
    merged with sunlight so a horsefly wheeled
blue-green in its own wingbeat
    by a rote it answered to in music,
lesser to the greater as the greater
    to the whole, tube twice bent
on itself, sine curve on the line of displacement,
    sending sound backwards until it's now?

5

William, when thirty kids try out for basketball
        calculate the odds, the tendency of mind
to see itself in transition — feminine green light
        like call waiting — you might be playing trumpet
into the speaker, your girlfriend Corrine might
        be listening, exhausting her telephone allotment
of fifteen minutes, holding her ear inches away, glint
        of a clipboard watching you both. You might move
                                                    out of
the paint. The yellow squeak of rubber on oak
        wakes rivers of grain — what does it matter
that this matter jumps back or breaks for open court —
        sometimes you only stand and scream,
wave both arms, put it on the floor and drive,
        lay it up, put it down, take it home.

6

Let me find the keys says Candace

    let's go says William the water

nibbles at the bank sunlight shafts

    the fog   wait says Candace

clouds back off the water

    what else the boat suspended

glint gray along the gunnels

    here they are I've found them

the washing machine idles in its cycle

    sun shattered in water slaps

let's go says William   the legs follow

    the surface tension   the door closes

the car starts the green wave slides

    under the boat   a day begins.

7

Slow it down, bring it down, bring it
      on home, tympanum of the trumpet-
flower, raised hood, swollen yellow face,
      pathological woe standing
in rank grass against the Hurricane fence,
      half a brick bewildered, half
carried through slatted shadows, cracked
      bell shrouded by buildings, doorways
listening, patiently waiting for someone to open
      a paper bag and bring out the horn
and this one time it sounds exactly like
      laughter, wind blows in your face,
from a high window in metallic light
      long green trumpets beat back rain.

8

When the instruments linger in the band room,
      snare leaning into itself,
tuba beached against green cinderblock,
      do they riff where a fault opens,
make a crazy line in space, does brass
      lie in bronze alloy, does longing
breathe in acoustic energy? Notes hang
      to the skirt of the bell
like a city of light for a moment.
      A tire spooks the gravel, you hear talk
about the weather, the leaning toward
      and then away. Pierce the blind
to better hear the music, the fall
      of each sound and pause between.

9

It damages people when they do not understand
      the healing power of friendship.
I am damaged. The left front light of my transport
      is out. A day doesn't pass. An hour
does not go by. There are minutes that glow
      in human flesh. A trumpet has a voice.
A place lives in music of people and time.
      These are not things I know.
Things of the air are also not thought of
      in time of need. That is why the passive
voice is so active in distortion, and well
      to note that a slur is more expressive
than a sharp note timed to surface admiration,
      though the fool in me shines to perfection.

10

Soft percussive no-look pass of summer,
       flexion of bell, white seed
of longing and forgetfulness — I remember
       stopping on the way home from school
at a car showroom, perching on vinyl I could smell
       thinking I don't belong here
and the place about to close. I hold the page
       of music so you can see it, William,
your face reddens, your foot taps eight times
       to push breath past unbelievable seconds,
a dandelion head floats out of sight
       senseless and alive, full of feather
and plume, empty to itself wherever
       it flies, drifting from its own heart.

11

The dog growls, a low unearthed intent stands
    up on the back of the neck — I am here and
somewhere else — back in time maybe, fingers
    tap the valves. Make two trumpets
of silver Yahweh said to Moses —
    and make them play flat and sharp notes
at the same time said Ornette Coleman,
    no loose lipping. Wake the memory.
Wake the present tense. The tongue wicks the mouth-
                            piece.
    Horripilates the cause. Lights up the argument.
A column of air moving through an empty place,
    three stops, an opening outward
toward no purpose or proof beyond the time
    when people will not hear it.

12

My father's there. Like fugitive dust
  seeping through cracks and keyholes in Oklahoma
in the early 30s. What happens when I try
  to hold him is my arms pass through air.
Goodbye goodbye to the river and to
  green metallic leaves. I leave
the darkness which sat on my shoulders
  for love talk and grace of music.
Still, there are strains of darkness
  dear to light. I found a photograph
under the couch. My father barbecuing
  chicken with his shirt off, skin brown
as a berry. Grinning from the other side.
  Into the lens. Of light and song.

II. Shout Trumpet

1

When passing the Trumpet in Zion Church,
    red brick soaked with morning rain,
four cars parked on slickened blacktop,
    marked yellow lines, redbud clusters,
heart-shaped lavender pods, I keep hearing
    my own minor key. Even so,
a person puts a thumb out, an awning
    cantilevers, traffic comes
to a rolling stop. Through an open window
    high bright notes clarify the air
back to March wind, locked doors, to those who
    have lost their love, decided
to go and not come back: the high C
    of incalculable motion.

2

At the Trumpet in Zion they do the laying
        on of hands — your long hair
passes over me, the purpose of
        the body hidden in the word.
Thinking nothing. Resembling an eighth note.
        If the rapture taketh then where
does the body go when hands lie down on air?
        A flag dragged through the iris
upside down. Desire runs through its stops —
        the dance rises to water level.
What happens inside music to make it run
        over arms and legs like a squirrel?
Toot toot go to the water to the river
        of folded wings,

3

where catalpa shade holds a body of gnats
     just the shape of smoke and water
saturates yellow air and a water moccasin
     displaces the imagination —
not away from but toward where the world
     reaches and a song carries across water,
one they've been singing all along,
     the same notes and fears,
the sound of pure tones. I wouldn't know it
     if I heard it. I might not
know if it were only mine.
     I would like to think I could clearly hear
the music as it calls across so
     I could know what you know.

4

Bats are back. Looping the Mulberry. Concentric
      gravitational waves. I think I notice
my own radar. I loll in a yellow chair
      with two ear plugs connected to Art Porter.
Art Porter Junior in background on clarinet.
      Little Rock's own. Follow the ogive turns
past Maybelline to Telegraph Road, past
      Jimmy Doyle's and the white birches,
signs for Alltel and Jesus, SunCom,
      and Ruby Lube. Are you a holy roller
William asks his grandmother. No but I'm
      spirit-filled. Her sisters' faces
ghost across her own face as it is — Jean,
      Billie in her garden, pious Lucille.

5

I ask myself riddles in sleep and part of me
      thinks it knows the answers. My
body leaks, my ignorance, my desire. I keep a
      gold tooth which is not the trumpet,
wood landing over water knock, photon locked
      in early light wrapped around
a cove, people in a boat, not much talking
      but it echoes, love is there, when
will I ever believe, fill the body up and sing.
      A wireless chip with beams of light carries
itself in your eye. Who sleeps upside down
      on a ledge with toes turned in, dreams of making
love mid-air, only you and me in water? Bats are back.
      I feel a scarf of air rush past.

6

Some mean ass little red bug just bit the shit out of me!
     So why does it grease the room with soulless
nasal noise, no antennae for opposites,
     alighting on the trumpet case? Seven years
of mending, leaving and coming back through you,
     I think I can hear syncopation
in the last half of the beat, cancellation
     too, but I only want to touch the button
on your blouse. The hi-hat clears the moment.
     Out of nowhere you came to me.
Where is memory with its leaning sideways solo
     under a stone weight? Out of nowhere
you came back. Today and today an old wind blows,
     music flares above the grasstips.

7

When the moon stares from its forehead
    and sound waves and particles
knock on tiny hairs in the inner ear,
    information travels — how can one not know
the only pressure occurs at a molecular
    level? A channel forms in the flow of ions.
When one whacks at a cloud of flies,
    one clarifies that insects don't know where
the hell they are — they can't hear
    right so spend their remaining days
complaining that music by itself is trivial.
    Their bristles get bent, ions
flow in to trumpet the brain, but still
    no hard high note, no upward rip.

8

Plumbline of the asters, music caught inside
    the throat, the implacability, the fluted crescent
of the body, the temple, the infarcted heart,
    the age of reason, the tap tap tap of the baton:
one time one steps off the porch two stories high,
    next the song sings itself:
the air, the ambient glue, the tongue
    in mid-salute, the coup de langue,
the nation at war, the wormhole connecting nothing
    to nothing, the creak of heaven over
the creek, the flat speckled rock, the event
    horizon, the accretion disk, the no
which means no, the wide swing under stars,
    the water, the verb, the hidden grammar.

9

Not long ago a fly landed in the butter.
    The buzz stumbled, the the stared out
from the portable computer, the astral light
    combined with the high speed line
to toot back an unheard, unseen opinion
    so popular here in the South.
I reach for you and nothing, not anything
    from all the days of walking, breathing
in and out, waking to change and resemblance,
    quickened to the task of words,
time and timing unsung — belly to belly,
    keyboard to hyperthought, one wing
gleaming on a salt sweet brick like a face
    in the screen, increased singularity.

10

I hear the neighbors talking over the fence —
     "He came driving up in that turd-colored
convertible and didn't even open the door
     when he saw his stuff all flayed out
in the bushes and grass, his shirt with the sleeve
     drooping over the hostas. . . ." The glass doors
screech, the monarch glisses over standing water,
     the ego in its drifting boat interminably waits.
We have no ideas but why should we say goodbye?
     The signature and sign don't mean
the end of it. White azalea blossom stuck to mud.
     That is the end of winter, this
a preoccupation with weather which has nothing
     more than last night on its mind.

11

Thunder and rain all day like the drumming
        of Zutty Singleton. Ivy gropes
the fern, a sprig of oak pollen navigates
        over two bar breaks. One or two
octaves over, like a ghost flattened out, down
        the basement, up one flight
to the dirty silver door with Judas hole, to a few
        tables and wicker chairs, late afternoon — that's
where to hear a phrase turn. The upright
        shakes the floor, and when
however fast the falling torrent flows —
        stop that please thinks management if people
stand too long and listen — the whole world knows
        in wind when self assured, the roses blow.

12

You know that silo in Oklahoma, the one with
       chipped tooth on the way to Grandma's house
where apple blossoms lit the way to certain hell?
       Well, it's gone now. The leaping light
and silence. Through channels of urgent voluntary
       sing-song, passing tones in the hallway
mirror, tension through the saunter of water cooled
       air, all is gone. You don't have to remember.
Only that violation in the upper registers which
       sounded and does sound in houses
just a few blocks over, and in fact, in this house
       which is hot at night and cunning,
waits for a future. Slap-tongue's gone. The mouth
       meets and notches the music.

III. Body and Soul

1

In summer all desires are known. Events
    lie everywhere. Time and measure
make a vee in the sky. Forgetting is still knowing.
    I think I might as well turn around and go back home —
to be part of the chromatic scale, orange dust.
    When you pass through you only know
you have passed through. A drowsiness
    in early afternoon assumes
a practical role, very different for different people.
    That might not sound right.
The problem is that there are things to do.
    Installations in momentum.
Peace of nodding branches, shade and light.
    Watching airplanes land.

2

Last night I woke thirteen times, rolled
      toward you then back, then toward,
then slid my hand between your biceps
    and ulna, sat up, searched
for something, a pretext for looking,
     an agency of improvisation
bending under the weight of eternity.
    In summer all secrets are hid,
encoded in thought like water music.
    One gets lost in the changes.
So much happens between worlds
    the movement seems circular,
reiterative like running rain catching up
    to recognize hydrogen.

3

In summer the doors and windows fly open,

       portals of the planet let go

their stay — time to blow the hinges off, rip

       the upper register, to unbutton

the blues of the arms, to mix rum with coconut,

       to look over the Texaco station and watch

heaven turn apricot, a storm headed down-

       town, a funnel cloud fronting lit

debris, precincts of cool air, pockets

       of long distance — sirens sound,

fever in the atmosphere, a slice

       of siding overtaking — such

is entreaty, casual prayer, willing

       suspension of confusion.

4

In summer a pattern emerges — music floats
　　　above rooftops like charcoal smoke
in the suburbs. In *After*, Roy Eldridge hits high F
　　　then low G. There are fast ways and slow ways,
but always, said Red Allen, always play
　　　without a mute. *"Play the horn wide
open; you cannot lie."* Lucent folds inside the ear
　　　like lover's breath, rippling sibilance —
every insistence, every willful prediction licking
　　　the oval window, every desire shaping
enchantment. Bones in the skull give back
　　　the voice; the ear trumpets in three parts,
the deepest bridged by three again.
　　　A high bright verb lights our passage.

5

I first heard an amplified chord in Jaymack
      Norwood's garage, the bald spot
of my fifth grade flattop an entry place for all
      influence, my satellite well-being determined
by infatuate stars, electric guitar combing my gooseflesh,
      my body awakening, *Pipeline*
morphing blank Oklahoma air —
      who else was there?
Jaymack's sister, Bobby Ragland . . . I don't know —
      I'm still in thrall, a vibration set
on air, invisible wave, so casually part
      of the chromatic scale I forgot
what I was talking about, what story-line brought
      daylight, cool concrete, chord-anchored.

6

Poor Oklahoma, surreal whistle-stop, wind
        and dust, particulate cloud — I'm glad
there's no speed limit on the Turnpike —
        blue stump nestled in grama, sparse
trees, tumbleweed flat against the fence, Coke
        stacked twelve crates high on a corner
Exxon lot — I remember your electric air,
        tornado country oil rich, trembling
panhandle, sulfur muck, sink hole,
        beer belly. I drink and drive over Tenkiller,
the shimmer of asphalt bespeaks distance,
        the elevation in language false, not
because words and the world refuse to blur —
        diesel fumes bloom on passing tones.

7

: that's what I heard.
          I blew into a comb wrapped

in cellophane — translucent corridors,

       locks and lockers, fluent slurs

like school, like years. Spooky air, cobweb

       we walk through, save us from particulars —

uh, I'll do the ride-out, you do slide

       piano . . . that hand of yours on mine:

is it because of something I said earlier,

       or the press of this moment?

I see that slide of eye like a deep star

       rolling under a granite wave

away from the upglint spinning debris

       one feels the pull of the surround of.

8

When Mingus dying of Lou Gehrig's
    disease sang from his high rise
just above the beat, starlight fissure, rain of
    willful syllable, that which does not belong
to powerful interests of the earth, I guess
    I must've been married and
divorced, hitchhiking through St. Louis,
    sleeping in beige stubble, cop
kicking me awake, once in the ribs
    so that my eyes opened with
knowledge that this was where some dream
    ended and the legs carried the body
away, away from people who would
    wonder why the body was there.

9

From rock my father lifted geological data
      raised out of earth smelling
like sea breezes, from out of need
      for air, salt for duration, animal
eyes for what seemed innocent. On a platform
      in a house where I sat with him
and watched as he drank from a steaming thermos
      and held and tasted rocks, the derrick
would sway against osage light, early morning —
      it seems strange to remember the way
he stood and held rocks to light and cursed
      information on the tongue.
From on top of a vibrating mesh structure
      I barely felt the fracture.

10

Put your face down to water, black rose
      of surfaces — out of cottonwood
lining nighttime gospel dirt roads
      you walked barefoot, if only
in dream — the Hammond organ, smell of
      sea salt — a selection always comes.
Ghost of this moment, this water,
      animal shape — it's always easy
to accuse, to hold back or press, praise
      difficulty, know more than this.
Someone always seems to know more . . .
      black flower poised above black
standing stretched-out tempo, water
      of resolve, flower of unresolve. . . .

11

That traffic hiss sounds like the work week.
Drop one boot. Go back to sleep.
Flatted fifth of three disappearing herons.
What do you think fell into
the field of milo out beyond the cleft?
Why crystallize one moment of
sound distribution? Go back to sleep,
one part body heat, two parts
marine shell distance — fundament and
firmament, the very place of
trumpets. Maybe one should drift on the lips
of whatever is playing so that the insult
of time and space renders unaware, unavailable
a conversion into work.

12

For all we know the inverse square law
    of the propagation of light
includes grain in a stairwell in
    a house in St. Joseph, Missouri.
Coleman Hawkins used to practice there.
    Body and Soul enraptures plaster,
each successive passing, and sometimes
    when two reveries touch
on a landing, a saxophone body calls,
    a glowing opening responds, a greeting conversation,
a dialogue, a mumbling forward, a lovemaking.
    Light kisses each eyelid,
a ghost note leans into an echo,
    for all we know.

II

For My Father-in-Law,
with a Last Line from Dante

You don't know what lovin is the old man said
        to his daughter, night air and windows down,
but she did. His head rolled along his shoulders
        when thunder made her move her head
toward his at the old folks home when she visited
        and they sat on the sofa in the waiting room
where the piano glistened like spit and urine.
        His head kept dropping to his chest,
he kept getting up and sitting back down, then
        up again to walk five steps, then down
to put out himself like a candle. The bracelet
        on his ankle set off waves to bolt the doors
but never got that close. For then would the feet
        be filled with good desire.

Food for Death

Come ham and cake, deviled eggs,
        pickled beets like blood to the brain,
floating orbs of meat, hoisted, carried
        at the level of thought near the ear
like waiters listening to food's music.
        Put it over there, clear
a space. The platter holds light.
        The tires punctuate the gravel road —
they will have to stop for cows
        who stare and stare as if somehow
a sudden movement backward
        never comes — Holstein art of surprise,
bottom land adrift. Come dry grits
        sprinkled with garlic amber like light
shooting through spirits aged
        five hundred thirty-seven miles northeast,
risen in yeast, or grease, lubrication
        just before it settles, half the moon
like a forehead with an idea.
        Everyone wants to go home. A bovine
plenitude exasperates the under-
        belly sweep. How much do I see?

Bread from the oven, wine

    (I wish there were wine), turkey overdone,

white as birches simplified, steepled

    in a clearing. This is the prelude to

a country funeral (the hicks say

    open the casket, the hicks say no),

death under the oat, the body put down, food

    for the planet, and stars, wine

of nonexisting rivers — may we drink to health

    and drink itself and all manner of beast fallen

in accord with noise and appetite, waves

    of fire, and weeping. Fart on you,

says a little boy to his sister; go

    to your room, says his mother.

Off go the lights; they all go

    flying down. Cake for death,

petroleum rainbow in the ham (I'll have

    a piece of that pie going by, said Elvis).

The black bottom land shifts in its tectonics;

    the mashed potatoes dance in red-eye gravy.

Is there a food for desire? Of course,

    there always is, always and forever

the salads, the vinaigrette, the the of the restaurant order,
		the wafer, the flaked Parmesan,
the very little ice in the nature of ferment,
		the lifted benefaction to the lips,
pouting lips, parted on the face of it. Frito pie,
		backbeat of peppercorn, King
Ranch casserole, buckets
		of chicken, seven-layer salad.
The peas are in a world of their own;
		the butter crashes on itself;
the Shamrock glasses wait as if to waltz;
		the forks hide among the knives and spoons —
the laughter of their parts, the touch, the old association,
		shines.

Boyish

I knocked three teeth down
the bulldog's throat, I know
by the way he choked
as I rattled clear of the fence,
my belly full of green peaches,
the sky riding changeless
oxytones, the gray nettles
stuck to my trouser legs.
Rocks and tree roots clogged
Bowman Acres and dead water
rose along my ankles. What is it
now in the door slamming
and floors shaking that resonates
so that someone seems always
to be leaving? Dark daylight hammers
on the roof until the house topples.
I knocked three times.
The dog raced along blue water,
picked up a bike chain and tossed it.
A water cooler pumped air
and water backward into
a dream of bluegrass.
I picked up a chair and knocked

the dog in the head, one tooth

hanging from a dark red

strand like a dragonfly.

Returning now I ask the clouds

for caution. I lie in state in a rubber raft

with gin balancing a coaster.

Cicadas vibrate, bats loop

and surrender. When the radio voice

rises in the lawn next door

I decide I am no longer young.

Highwater fear, I can see

my plunder, though I never

was there, or anywhere.

Back

I can hear the even clicking
of a bluejean button as it tumbles

in the clothes dryer in a room
off the kitchen. Is the world

coming to an end? Why ask
such questions if it is not?

The lucid skin, the salt and sorrow.
I am back in childhood.

I see the father leaning over the steaks.
He has his shirt off, is smiling into the lens.

He thinks he will never die.
The stars in heaven shake their chains.

Smoke rises like always with casual
meandering florets which stick in the eye.

The mother seeks unintended grace.
Unintended? Grace? Seeks?

I have been this child who hid.
Who listens as the button falls.

*

If you turn away the universe
would sail, everything would

shift. The moment pressing down.
In a few minutes the telephone rings.

The voice says who in hell
do you think you are.

If I bother to look outside
snow sluices down the street

with great masses of leaves
I haven't raked but I stare

inward and fail to speak
as if I'm on a bus.

The setting spins by.
The dwellings are real.

I am who I think.

Wildflowers of the Western World

What pops up out of space from thin green
        stalks soothes the eye,
a risen green that travels toward
        unindentured light. Imagine
that, and white around the edges as the days,
        crimson (I think) in the center
with a scent so deep the life seems
        deeper where the labor goes.
Take them like the head of a beast.
        Or let them lean on air.
Allow or don't allow the words
        foot-candle or crow foot, white
petals at midnight after the thought
        swims through the body.

That's a celebration. Unlike the mood
        of the Spurge family, particularly
Sally Spurge who squats in public
        and effuses a milky juice.
Their stamens and pistils rise from
        short stalks. Or the moccasin
flower with its lethal verbal tradition.
        It's hard to believe the veiny
slipper with its crease along
        the front. Suppose spurred orchids

clamored toward showy spikes in
    blue clay, and Sally stood by
with her large, culpable hands, and the
    window overturned at mom's house.

The naked miterwort came by today
    with a load of those wonderful
tomatoes. One couldn't tell
    fragrant bedstraw from the rough
bedstraw, though the leaves ascended
    from their stems. The tumblemustard,
that wild sensitive plant from
    Kansas, poked through, saying something
singular, but it sounded like howdy there.
    The erect bugle was the last to leave
with blue-eyed Mary. I saw them
    walking then flying, then
the ground turned to pudding under
    the nipplewort, most perverse of all flowers.

When a star streaks
    someone is dying but when
a thistle stitches itself to
    an ovoid under starlike

starts here is the cup,

      the yellow filament, here

are the relatively short spurs,

      the conscious recollection, here

is the reenactment of

      inadequacy which is

language, a history shorter

      than the fringes around my lip.

Loose thread on the margins.

Once I rode a bicycle

      across Tulsa, Oklahoma

and swooned in heat stroke

      like a day lily but still

the climate, how shall I say,

      levitated like charcoal smoke

over steak — it went on up

      the channel of hurt and want.

The beauty of the beauty

      of the beauty is that

wildflowers are too direct —

      something in their disposition

smiles at the earnest truth.

III

Comfort Inn

Last night through the motel room
     wall I heard a woman's
cry — her direction to whoever
     pursued, rhetorical shiver of air
caught in the night, visible lace
     around the moon, continental
shift of the face. This morning two boys
     slapped water with a fin.
This is the sound, one boy said,
     of a man hitting a woman;
this is the sound of a woman hitting
     a man. The motel pool glitters,
sparks fly out of the flesh.
     I would recede from joy or dream
the dream I cannot avoid.
     Was it love or its opposite,
the muffled voice? I think
     I heard Security outside, the radio
static, blue flash cascading
     night air; but soon the noise recurred,
its tongue like a flame in the mouth.
     The sound seemed mixed, the love

and the hate, the woman

      under the man, the cries of unbelief

or ecstasy or wound. I think of them

      now driving north, up through Kentucky

to Indiana and whether or not the woman's

      okay and the limit of my concern.

The things I forget wheel above me.

      White seeds float in blue air,

holes in Maytime sailing,

      land in yellow grass, lend an efflorescence

to the surface tension of water.

Lamentations

...sitting in forgotten chairs ... (Paul Zweig)

You dang near pulled my finger off says
      my neighbor to her dog
and her dog stares briefly and breaks.
      She's recently married to her
second husband, Gerald, the happiness
      new and dramatic, but there are pains, or numb-
                    nesses,
her whole left side seems half
      alive, the cervical area, she
points with her right arm and forefinger
      behind her neck, this might be it. . . .
Her dog has stopped and stands still
      as if straddling two cities.
The insolent white star of his chest.
      The love of sitting in forgotten chairs.
The laughter of two people, the
      yield, the humility
endlessly.

Not the boredom and fear,
      not the waiting, not the motion
and momentum. Only
      the spokelike tender turnings like

a bicycle clicking through time.
The pain situates here
and here, the left holds on to
the right, the dog has
flown to what he imagines
as the final spectra —
where else would one wear a leash
over the shoulder
like a scarf on an airman?

Swamp Gas

Green as my hatred layered in fathoms,
lowered in shallow graves
    along the Delta, rising
like ghosts who will not speak,
    swamp candles line the runway,
wildflowers with yellow tongues grace
    silk air. What is the South that I worship
like wallpaper too bright and hurtful?
    The fog-filled bottom takes me down
to my knees, the falling off
    curls in on itself like the snail
whose feet go slowly fast.
    I sense a compulsion as I walk, gasoline
surge of heat in the sidewalk. The grasses
    never grow above the waist, the light
ticks too close to the ground.
    Drinking beer with that film over the pitcher
like humidity in the South at night,
    I remember the dead man's float
of unfathomable grass.
    How the light seemed to smoke.
Don't call it wisdom, atmosphere, or slow
    dissolve, light prismed

to a feather. The blacktop slickens to an
　　　　emblem, the nostalgic figure props itself
on one elbow, mouth wide open in blackness,
　　　　face screwed to attention,
wings grown out of its throat
　　　　like a yucca moth. There is no end
to it, there is always an end,
　　　　the cropped yellow weave of the bermudas,
the blister of light which
　　　　seems a welcoming, the smack
of news against the door,
　　　　landed on a porch in a neighborhood
wakening in parts, creaking to dress
　　　　or undress, seeking to understand
and love again, to do harm
　　　　or violence, to do good,
to live from the heart
　　　　with the heart in mind.

Oil Well, Oklahoma

I remember watching my father taste rock
cut by a hollow drill, raised from a tray
of ultraviolet light. Say
you can measure the speed of sound, wake
that travels down and down
then refracts, then
smell it, the undetected radical
heave, buckle and distortion. When
it gets up here you can
taste it already, you can turn at odd angles
of your living like the muscular
live oak. Where
we swam the pit reeked,
a slant of strata was a sight of seepage,
shock waves struck
the horizon in zigzags.
Human persistence was powerless
in a sudden shift of wind.
The light traveled alone.
I had forgotten how the curtain
parted against basalt sky,
how carbon formed
a chain, why some

wells are

drilled for petroleum and some

for information.

Look this is easy said

my brother swinging

out over brown brack

and now I know —

it was easy.

If I had placed the hidden

ladder under grapevine

and gained a certain balance

then climbed like rust

through the stalk

I could've skated out of the clouds

like an orange mouse,

I could've skimmed over

water and landed

on clay and felt my feet

disappear.

Orphans Eating Sugar

You'd think they'd rot from inside out,
     their grained fingers hoisting stolen
sweetness, ingestion of an institution —
     you'd think they'd rot from inside out.
Their chairs squeak and knock on linoleum.
     The older boys smoke on the screened
smoke porch, cold even in late spring,
     yellow smoke scallops, circling rivers,
ascending white blossoms, narcissus narcosis.
     They stare out at traffic like glass horses,
distrust all who have dominion, including themselves,
     whose teeth rock free from their cradles,
who grind enamel down to know the bite, the ache,
     to lie down in the hole they make.

We Are Seven

A woman in Mexico thought she was having septuplets
        but only a shadow on the ultrasound made seven —
I've heard the descriptions of swimming in the womb
        before time like waving grass.
When I took the bus home from Hamilton Junior High
        I balanced myself in the aisle,
I brushed up against bodies until it was time
        to sit, I gripped my books and choked
an empty paper sack. The bus driver had a cowlick
        which stared from the rearview.
I have always been respectful of the unborn
        it seemed to say from the olive oil,
I cannot speak in ways that they remember,
        I do not now. The late grey sky of the fifties
seemed always to be in motion, as if the clouds
        were stuck in helical grooves.
Who were its parents? Was Sputnik still rising
        beyond the moon with its spikes
glistening from moisture exuded from the stars?
        My parents would be each preparing
for the evening when one would raise a hand
        and the other cower. . . .

What is the time you most remember?

    Six inches away from the wall I see you

hanging from a stranded wire with others who

    look like you staring out of non-glare glass

at the outside which is inside looking in

    at how your arms droop, how your whole

tribe matches itself to high water —

    there is no air conditioning —

the hair speaks from the head with finality

    of the soul; the family of being sits

in darkness on a wall, heads bowed, knives

    and forks at ready, impatient for grace.

Notes

"Ghost Notes," technically, are notes more implied than actually played. Thanks to my wife Candace and my son William for allowing me to appropriate them for this poem. The last line of Section 8 owes to Thomas Hardy's "The Moon Looks In." In Section 12, the phrase "strains of darkness dear to light" comes from a hymn. Part 2, Section 2, out of context, is a private and frankly sentimental nod to Dick Hugo, "Toot toot." Part 3, Section 8 refers to Charles Mingus' part singing and humming, barely audible "Chair in the Sky" which his wife recorded in their high rise near the end of his life. Danny Fletcher, to whom "Ghost Notes" is dedicated, is a band teacher at Mann Junior High School in Little Rock, who taught my son how to play trumpet and who is the most generous, dedicated teacher I have ever known.

I also owe special thanks to readers of the title poem, "Ghost Notes," particularly to David Young, Paul Zimmer, Candace Burns, Lisa Lewis, Dave Jauss, Lesha Hurliman, Daryl Rice, Rene Arehart, Mary Lambright, and Adam Giannelli. Additional thanks to the Office of Research and Sponsored Programs at the University of Arkansas at Little Rock for a grant during the writing of these poems.

Acknowledgments

Some of these poems have appeared in the following magazines, which I gratefully acknowledge for their support:

BRILLIANT CORNERS: "Ghost Notes," under the title "Pure Tones"

CIMARRON REVIEW: "Wildflowers of the Western World"

FIELD: "Boyish," "Lamentations"

NORTH DAKOTA QUARTERLY: "We Are Seven"

POETRY INTERNATIONAL: "Comfort Inn"

SOLO: "Oil Well, Oklahoma," "Swamp Gas"

SYCAMORE REVIEW: "For My Father-in-Law, with a Last Line from Dante"

Special thanks to painter Stephen Henriques, whose "Fra Angelico Meets Ornette Coleman" graces the cover.